YOUR KNOWLEDGE HAS VALUE

- We will publish your bachelor's and master's thesis, essays and papers

- Your own eBook and book - sold worldwide in all relevant shops

- Earn money with each sale

Upload your text at www.GRIN.com
and publish for free

Bibliographic information published by the German National Library:

The German National Library lists this publication in the National Bibliography; detailed bibliographic data are available on the Internet at http://dnb.dnb.de .

This book is copyright material and must not be copied, reproduced, transferred, distributed, leased, licensed or publicly performed or used in any way except as specifically permitted in writing by the publishers, as allowed under the terms and conditions under which it was purchased or as strictly permitted by applicable copyright law. Any unauthorized distribution or use of this text may be a direct infringement of the author s and publisher s rights and those responsible may be liable in law accordingly.

Imprint:

Copyright © 2019 GRIN Verlag
Print and binding: Books on Demand GmbH, Norderstedt Germany
ISBN: 9783668972759

This book at GRIN:

https://www.grin.com/document/488791

Christoph Grube

Mother to child transmission of HIV in Sub-Saharan Africa

Challenges and barriers that prevent a decline

GRIN - Your knowledge has value

Since its foundation in 1998, GRIN has specialized in publishing academic texts by students, college teachers and other academics as e-book and printed book. The website www.grin.com is an ideal platform for presenting term papers, final papers, scientific essays, dissertations and specialist books.

Visit us on the internet:

http://www.grin.com/

http://www.facebook.com/grincom

http://www.twitter.com/grin_com

Mother to child transmission of HIV in sub-Saharan Africa,

Challenges and barriers that prevent a decline

Christoph Grube

Ludwig-Maximilians-University Munich

The first formally recognized finding of human immunodeficiency virus (HIV) in patients in 1981 in the USA and its spread across the globe started one of the biggest research topics of human medicine. What is often referred to as acquired immune deficiency syndrome (AIDS) is a complex and divers' system of viruses. HIV strains collected from all around the globe have shown to have a large variety. Human immunodeficiency virus type 1 (HIV-1), the retrovirus that affects humans, can be separated into three subcategories. The first being group N and O, which are rarer than the most common strain, group M. This group is found in an estimated 98% of all HIV-infected around the globe (Sharp & Hahn, 2010). Sub-Saharan countries still have an unproportional part of the global HIV infection compared to the rest of the globe. In 2013 Sub-Saharan countries, despite only being home to around 12% of the global population, have been estimated to account for almost 71% of global HIV infections. The most common form of getting infected by HIV is by heterosexual contact, followed by mother to child transmissions (MTCT). Women are disproportionately affected by HIV. 58% percent of people living with HIV are women (Kharsany & Karim, 2016) and young women are twice as likely to acquire HIV as their male counterparts (UNAIDS (2), 2017). Antiretroviral therapy (ART) has made living with HIV possible. The once fatal disease can be treated with medicine, that allows an almost normal life by suppressing the virus and even vertical transmission can be prevented. The increasing availability of such drugs has caused a decline in AIDS related deaths in sub-Saharan regions over the years of around 39% from 2005 to 2013, however the total number of these deaths is still high, especially compared to other regions of the globe (Kharsany & Karim, 2016). ART coverage increased significantly in east and west African regions from around 24% to 54% from 2010 to 2015. Over 10.3 million people were reached with that treatment (Department of Health, 2015).

Even with the slowly declining numbers of infected people and people with no access to treatments this still is a big issue that should be tackled and done more research on, especially the mother to child transmission of HIV. MTCT contributes largely to the number of children affected by HIV by the age of ten and under. Estimates say around 1600 children infected by HIV get born every day with a large proportion of them in sub-Saharan regions. Whilst in developed countries different treatments before, during and after birth have decreased transmission rates from 25-30% down to less than 2%, countries in the sub-Saharan area do not show such declining numbers due to social, cultural and economic barriers (McIntyre & Gray, 2009).

This paper aims to point out why this should be worked on more and why factors like education and reducing social stigma should be advanced in order to enable a faster decline of vertical transmission numbers. As the numbers above show, MTCT is still an issue in sub-Saharan countries that must be addressed. Furthermore, this paper is going to explain how the basic mechanisms of MTCT work and how it possibly can be prevented in every stage of the pregnancy. Furthermore, this paper tries to explain why social, cultural and economic factors play such a big role in fighting against HIV and are challenges that must be tackeld. By the end it should be clear, how all these factors tie together and what future research could be done in order to reduce the numbers of people getting affected by HIV and especially infants and young people.

The mechanisms of vertical transmission

In 2015 the Department of Health of South Africa conducted a study to determine the number of women attending public sector antenatal clinics in south Africa, which were HIV positive. In South Africa around 30.8% of these women were HIV positive with large regional differences from 18.9% in West Cape up to 44.4% in KwaZulu-Natal (Department of Health, 2015).

Due to the lack of prevention of MTCT, around one third of these women will infect their children with HIV-1 (McIntyre & Gray, 2009). From this research it is explained how children can get infected in three ways: before the child is born in utero, during the birth and postnatally. The risk of getting infected in each of those stadiums is influenced by various factors.

The risk before the child's birth, for example, is influenced by factors like clinical chorio-amnionitis, which is an inflammation of the placenta or the placental membrane that has shown to lead to a significantly higher rate of vertical transmission. But other factors like maternal cigarette smoking or intravenous drug use during the pregnancy have also shown some evidence to have an effect on MTCT (McIntyre & Gray, 2009). Another decisive factor that influences the risk of an infection is a low cluster of differentiation 4-level (CD4). CD4 in general is a measurement of how well your immune system is operating. Individuals, who are affected by HIV, have a low count, usually between 200-500, while healthy individuals have a number between 500-1200 ("CD4 count or T-cell count", n.d.).

During the birth the child can be infected by getting in contact with blood or other secretes that contain the virus by small wounds or breaks in the skin. Also, the risk during birth is heavily influenced by the mode of delivery. An analysis of over 8500 births showed that woman who delivered their child with elective caesarean section reduced the risk of perinatal transmission by 50%. Twin birth children have shown to have different chances of getting infected based on the order in which the children are born. The first child has an infection rate of 35%, while the second child only has an infection rate of 15%. Caesarean section delivery can lower these numbers from 35% to 16% and from 15% to 8%.

But even after the delivery children can infected with HIV. The most prominent factor for this is breastfeeding, which alone has been associated with an additional risk of 14-18% (McIntyre & Gray, 2009).

Prevention possibilities of mother to child transmission

In 1983 the first 21 infants with unexplainable immunodeficiency were found. This seemed to be the first evidence that HIV-1 could be passed on from infected mothers to their children (Centers for Disease Control and Prevention, 1983). Since then there has been a significant advance in the treatment, which has made a vertical transmission – in theory – very unlikely. However, this advance has only shown its real effects in the developed countries, while developing countries, which often have a large HIV burden, have not experienced much benefit from those advancements in medicine, as it can be seen in the difference in the earlier mentioned transmission rates. Only half of the women in sub-Saharan Africa, who are infected with HIV, get an ART treatment to prevent MTCT in the first place (Ondenge et al., 2014).

The prevention of the transmission has made a lot of progress ever since the first infants with HIV were found. For every stage that allows MTCT (in utero, birth, breastfeeding) different treatments have been found and developed over time.

Pre-pregnancy and family planning

The first step of preventing MTCT is even before pregnancy; by possibly preventing the pregnancy itself. Many prevention programs encourage women, who are tested HIV positive, to limit the number of unwanted children. Unwanted pregnancies play a big role in the number of HIV positive infants, as a 2014 study about the sexual and reproductive health of HIV positive women found out. Nearly 60% of the participants said they had at least one unwanted pregnancy (Salamander Trust, 2014). Sub-Saharan countries do not only have the highest number of HIV individuals, but also the highest unmet need for contraception. About 20% of women in those regions have reported to have an unmet need for contraceptives (UNFPA, 2016). Despite integrating family planning services into HIV care and treatment services, there has yet been found no statistically significant evidence, that this had a positive influence on reducing unintended pregnancy, although these programs provide modern contraceptive methods and knowledge about the dangers of pregnancies with HIV (Haberlen, Narasimha, Beres & Kennedy, 2017).

Prevention in utero

As earlier mentioned, the CD4 count in the blood is linked to the risk of a vertical transmission. ARTs have made it possible to suppress the viral load in the blood, thus making a transmission more unlikely. ART programs have made a huge progress since more and more countries implemented protection of mother to child programs (PMTCT) into their healthcare systems. In 2014, 21 sub-Saharan countries provided ARTs to 77% of women living with HIV compared to 37% in 2009. This shows a good progress towards total ART cover, however, some countries still struggle to provide ART treatments on a national level, like Ethiopia, which implemented free ARTs in 2005 but still struggled to provide them in 2015 (UNAIDS, 2015).

Prevention during and after birth

One big step in preventing MTCT during the birth is by using elective caesarean section. As mentioned above, this has severe advantages compared to a natural birth, since the risk of the infant getting in touch with blood or other secretes that contains the virus is heavily reduced.

However, one of the biggest parts in preventing a vertical transmission starts after birth. The 2017 progress report by UNAIDS has stated, that about half of the infections that occurred that year, happened during breastfeeding. One of the biggest challenges is keeping the women with HIV in an effective ART treatment (UNAIDS, 2017). It seems that many women stop taking their ARTs after they give birth. The WHO gave different guidelines over the years on how to minimize the risk of vertical transmission, based on new findings in medicine. The general conduct was to avoid breastfeeding, if possible. However, in some regions this might not be an option due to various factors, like unavailability of certain replacement feedings. For women who had to breastfeed, the WHO set up a guideline on which medicine should be taken. One of the first effective medicine, that was found, was called Nevapirine in 1999 and it reduced the risk of vertical transmission by nearly 50% during the first 14-16 weeks after birth on breastfed children (Guay et al.,1999). But, as we have seen, widespread supply of such medicine did not happen until the mid 2000s and is still not available everywhere today. In 2011, 35 countries at the UN decided a global plan on elimination of MTCT. Target of this plan are low- and middle-income countries, like Ethiopia and other sub-Saharan countries, which account for most HIV positive children. The main goals were to reduce HIV related deaths of infants by more than 50% and providing ART for all mothers and infected children in order to reduce HIV infections of infants by 90% (UNAIDS, 2015). As a UNAIDS report shows, their measurements seemed effective, at least in adult HIV patients. In 2018, the AIDS-related deaths were at a decade record low, with fewer than one million people dying of AIDS-related illness and over 21 million people on treatment, over two million more than in 2016. However, their set goal of reducing infant infections for 2018 was missed and only half of under 15-year old's were on treatment by 2017 (UNAIDS (3), 2018).

Barriers on accessing ART

With the previous numbers in mind the question arises, why the numbers for children and young people have such trouble on declining. The answer to this question is far more complex than it might seem at first glance. There are different hurdles that have to be taken in order to give more people, especially HIV positive mothers and children, access to ARTs. A 2017 study about patient- reported barriers, conducted in 24 sub-Saharan countries, found that patients experienced 43 possible barriers in accessing ART (Croome, N., Ahluwalia, M., Hughes, L. D., & Abas, M., 2017).

One of the first big barriers is knowing your HIV status first. Many women in sub-Saharan areas don't even make a test to determine if they are infected or not. Numbers of pregnant women getting tested vary vastly between the different regions and countries. In 2018, 75% of people with HIV were aware of their HIV status in the total region of sub-Saharan countries, however there are regions where the numbers are significantly lower. In some western and central African regions, the numbers go as low as 48%, which shows the huge gap between the regions.

This leaves over nine million people not knowing their status in total in sub-Saharan regions, which is especially problematic for women who are getting pregnant (UNAIDS (2), 2018). The knowledge factor is especially problematic for children. Multiple visits to a testing facility are required to determine if a child or infant is HIV positive. Furthermore, many infants cannot start treatment until their second or third month of life, which is the period of peak mortality. Without treatment, 50% of the newborn will die before their second birthday (UNAIDS (2), 2017)

Social and cultural barriers

Despite more and more hospitals offer HIV testing, stigma and social barriers still play a large role on preventing pregnant women, or people in general, from using them. Often times women fear social consequences, if they are tested positive and their family members or friends get to know about it, or simply if they are seen visiting a hospital to get tested. This gets amplified, if laws like the "HIV Prevention and AIDS Control Bill" in Uganda in 2014 get passed, which criminalizes the spread of HIV and allows doctors to disclose a person's HIV status to their partners or their family without their consent. Facts like this fuel the estimates, that around 50% of vertical transmissions can be attributed to stigma (ICRW, 2014). The options of getting tested are often referred to as opt-in and opt-out. Opt-in means the person that suspects being HIV positive takes the step to visit a hospital and get tested. Opt-out means the test is done automatically, if you visit the hospital to do other tests, like prenatal screenings for pregnant women, except you explicitly wish to be not tested. Fact is, many women wish to be tested during their pregnancy, however, some countries, like Uganda made testing mandatory for pregnant women, if they visit a hospital during their pregnancy. The ICRW report further warns about such steps. It may shy women away from getting antenatal care at all, which not only has a negative impact on vertical transmission rates, but could have negative effects on the pregnancy in total (ICRW, 2014). Although many countries have passed laws to protect people from getting discriminated due to their HIV status, however, many still don't trust those laws, which are often not taken too seriously anyways. Keeping in mind, that your HIV status can lead to social rejection, violence or even criminal prosecution, the possible consequences of taking a HIV test can seem to be worse than the consequences of not getting tested (UNAIDS (2), 2018).

Cultural beliefs and traditional gender roles also play a big role. In many sub-Saharan countries the traditional, male dominant gender roles are still common. Women in many of these counties still need the consent of their husbands or fathers to do simple things, like opening a bank account or buying things. But even worse is the fact, that women need this consent to access certain health services. This means the man takes the decisions, if the woman should get tested or take any further treatments, if they are tested positive. Again, this varies from region to region, but there are countries, Senegal, for example, were as low as 5% of women attending such services told they have the final say in their own health care. This is made possible by a lack of law and legal policies that would allow women to do such (UNAIDS (2), 2017).

Discrimination based on diversity and gender identity. There has been evidence that women, who use drugs, are sex workers or individuals who are lesbian, gay, bisexual, transgender and intersex (LGBTI) face more and sometimes more difficult to overcome barriers, that prevent them from getting into proper HIV care systems. Especially in sub-Saharan areas LGBTI persons seem to have lower education as a result of discrimination, bullying and violence (UNAIDS, 2018). But even if they get into such HIV programs, the discrimination does not stop. A study has shown, that the fear of discrimination within the health care system goes so far, that 10-40% of gay men in Burkina Faso, Côte d'Ivoire, Eswatini and Lesotho avoid or delay health care due to fear of stigma from healthcare providers (UNAIDS 2018). Another problem is, that many healthcare providers are not informed properly about the anatomy and the handling of LGBTI individuals, as a South African trans woman stated in an interview:

> "As a trans woman, healthcare providers do not have the correct information about my body. I experience that they are very uncomfortable dealing with a woman who have a penis. Some of they also wants to lecture me that what im doing – having sex with men – are wrong. They always want to preach me about how I will burn in hell. Now I avoid such centers."
>
> (Salamandertrust, 2014)

Although the UN Human Rights Council has taken efforts in the last few years to fight this kind of discrimination by calling all states to act forcefully to end violence and discrimination against people based on their gender and sexual orientation. However, the discrimination seems to persist. This shows that social stigma cannot be fought effectively by changing laws alone. There has to be done more, like implementing knowledge about LGTBI into school sex education, so that the stigma can be slowly but effectively be reduced.

Economic barriers

The next big barrier, besides cultural and social ones, are economic barriers. Economic factors can range from the general lack of education and health infrastructure to the direct costs of tests and treatments. Education plays an important role in general health and especially the sexual and reproductive health. Data has shown, that women with lower education are less likely to have their sexual and reproductive health needs met. Education also allows women to access information about health, which allows them to be more in control over their reproductive lives (UNAIDS, 2018). However, often times women are denied or limited in their access to education, which can be partly traced back to the traditional gender roles, despite access to education and reproductive health has been declared as a human right by the United Nations Special Rapporteur (UN Human Rights Council, 2010). One big step that has been taken, is the implementation of sex education in schools. Studies in low- and middle-income countries have shown that school-based sex education had a positive effect on knowledge about HIV and its risks. This education has shown to lead to the more frequent use of condoms and having fewer sexual partners, thus reducing their risk of getting infected by HIV (Fonner et al., 2014). However, the total use of condoms still remains relatively low, which is partly due to the distribution of condoms. Again, this varies from country to country. In some countries like Namibia and South Africa up to 40 condoms per male are available, while in some countries supplies goes as low as only five condoms per male in Angola or South Sudan. Furthermore, only 50% of males in 23 sub-Saharan countries reported to have used a condom during their last sexual intercourse (UNAIDS (2), 2017).

This shows that general health system barriers also play a role. There are still areas where treatments like ARTs are not available in every hospital or shortages in supply occur. Besides education, the individual costs that occur when seeking for testing or treatment have also shown to have an important role. The further a hospital, and therefore the access to HIV testing and ART is, or the more treatment costs, the more unlikely it gets that people use these services by themselves. Sub-Saharan Africa, where large parts are still rural, often lack in density of such services. The further away a clinic is, the bigger are the transportation costs and the time needed to get there.

Also, access to these treatments is sometimes not guaranteed by the government. However, money does not seem to play a big role in accessing ART, since many of the drugs are provided for free by the government with the help of other countries and NGOs (Posse, Meheus, Van Asten, Van Der Ven & Baltussen, 2008). While the whole region of sub-Saharan countries in total make a good progress towards providing everyone access to ARTs, there are still some regions with worse access than others. Countries like Botswana, South Africa and Zambia are providing better treatment access than other countries, like Nigeria or Central African Republic, where as few as 25% of the adult population has access to ARTs (Kharsany & Karim, 2016).

Conclusion and future research options

While the general medical aspects of HIV are clear by now, besides how to heal infected persons completely, there has still a lot of research to be done.
Especially the research on education, how to implement sexual education in schools covering all regions and how it can help improving eliminating stigma in societies has to be done, because, as we have seen, knowledge about HIV and its consequences plays a big role in preventing people from accessing ART or seeking for help in the first place.
Changing the regulations and laws helps on paper, however, changing a society's perception cannot be changed like laws overnight. As stated above, stigma still is one of the top reasons why people are not attending HIV services, especially LGBTI people. One solution that could be implemented, in order for people who fear the social consequences just because they want

to get tested, could be the widespread use of self-testing kits which could increase the reach of certain key populations like LGBTI. Research could be done on the effect and willingness to test themselves with HIV kits.

Reducing social stigma has to be a continuous process of influencing especially younger generations on how to handle the epidemic and its consequences and especially stop discrimination of key populations, like LGBTI people. Laws still need to be changed in various regions and countries to archive better supply, stop further discrimination and most importantly, allow women, who are still patronized by their husbands and fathers, to seek for help on their own and not be stopped from possibly saving their or their children's life just because someone tells them to. Social and cultural barriers need to be abolished in the long run.

Further research also should focus on how to improve economic variables, like making a wide spread of condoms standard, especially in those areas, where condoms or contraceptives in general are short on supply. In order to tackle all these barriers, studies should be conducted where participants are asked to rank the barriers by their importance in order for NGOs or governments to see which barriers need more attention or can be tackled in a cooperative work. People in studies have been frequently asked what barriers they face, but not which they think is the hardest to overcome.

This also should be done in a periodic study in order to see which measurements show effectiveness and should be taken further or what can be done to improve them. Since sub-Saharan countries are very different in their effectiveness of fighting the HIV problem, as we have seen in the regional differences in numbers like people attending health services or condom use, there needs to be more multilateral and international action to fight the problem effectively. Measurements up to this date, especially the reports of UNAIDS, which show that some problems like infants getting infected with HIV, are not declining at the levels to reach the set goals by the end of 2020 show, that there is still a lot of work to be done. The numbers are slowly declining, however, not at a rate on which they should and could. It is very important to see, that many of the factors that have an influence on the slow decline are tied together. Knowledge about HIV, for example, can be improved by education, which further can help improve reducing the social stigma. Education always seems to have a very important role on a nations wellbeing and should be therefore be one of the top priorities.

References

CD4 count (or T-cell count). (n.d.) Retrieved from
https://www.hiv.va.gov/patient/diagnosis/labs-CD4-count.asp

Centers for Disease Control and Prevention. Current Trends Acquired Immunodeficiency Syndrome (AIDS) Update - United States. MMWR Weekly 1983; 32(24):309-11.

Croome, N., Ahluwalia, M., Hughes, L. D., & Abas, M. (2017, April 24). Patient-reported barriers and facilitators to antiretroviral adherence in sub-Saharan Africa. AIDS. Lippincott Williams and Wilkins. https://doi.org/10.1097/QAD.0000000000001416

Fonner VA, Armstrong KS, Kennedy CE, O'Reilly KR, Sweat MD (2014) School Based Sex Education and HIV Prevention in Low- and Middle-Income Countries: A Systematic Review and Meta-Analysis. PLoS ONE 9(3): e89692. doi:10.1371/journal.pone.0089692

Fonner, V. A., Armstrong, K. S., Kennedy, C. E., O'Reilly, K. R., & Sweat, M. D. (2014). School based sex education and HIV prevention in low and middle-income countries: A systematic review and meta-analysis. PLoS ONE, 9(3). https://doi.org/10.1371/journal.pone.0089692

Guay, L. A., Musoke, P., Fleming, T., Bagenda, D., Allen, M., Nakabiito, C., ... Jackson, J. B. (1999). Intrapartum and neonatal single-dose nevirapine compared with zidovudine for prevention of mother-to-child transmission of HIV-1 in Kampala, Uganda: HIVNET 012 randomised trial. Lancet. https://doi.org/10.1016/S0140-6736(99)80008-7

Haberlen, S. A., Narasimhan, M., Beres, L. K., & Kennedy, C. E. (2017). Integration of Family Planning Services into HIV Care and Treatment Services: A Systematic Review. Studies in family planning, 48(2), 153-177.

Kharsany, A. B. M., & Karim, Q. A. (2016). HIV Infection and AIDS in Sub-Saharan Africa: Current Status, Challenges and Opportunities. The Open AIDS Journal, 10(1), 34–48. https://doi.org/10.2174/1874613601610010034

McIntyre, J. A., & Gray, G. E. (2009). Preventing mother-to-child transmission of HIV. In HIV Prevention (pp. 472–497). Elsevier Inc. https://doi.org/10.1016/B978-0-12-374235-3.00017-0

Ondenge, K., Voss, J., John-Stewart, G., Mills, L. A., Okanda, J., Kinuthia, J., … Odhiambo, F. (2014). Shame, Guilt, and Stress: Community Perceptions of Barriers to Engaging in Prevention of Mother to Child Transmission (PMTCT) Programs in Western Kenya. AIDS Patient Care and STDs, 28(12), 643–651. https://doi.org/10.1089/apc.2014.0171

Posse, M., Meheus, F., Van Asten, H., Van Der Ven, A., & Baltussen, R. (2008, July). Barriers to access to antiretroviral treatment in developing countries: A review. Tropical Medicine and International Health. https://doi.org/10.1111/j.1365-3156.2008.02091.x

Salamander Trust (2014). Building a safe house on firm ground: key findings from a global values and preferences survey regarding the sexual and reproductive health and human rights of women living with HIV

Sharp, P. M., & Hahn, B. H. (2010, August 27). The evolution of HIV-1 and the origin of AIDS. Philosophical Transactions of the Royal Society B: Biological Sciences. Royal Society. https://doi.org/10.1098/rstb.2010.0031

National department of health. (2015). The 2015 National Antenatal Sentinel HIV & Syphilis Survey. Retrieved from http://www.hst.org.za/publications/NonHST%20Publications/hiv_aids_survey.pdf

UN Human Rights Council (2010). Report of the Special Rapporteur on the right to education, Addendum: Communications sent to and replies received from Governments. 17 May 2010, A/HRC/14/25/Add.1. Retrieved from: http://www.unhcr.org/refworld/docid/4c29b2342.html.

UNAIDS (2). (2017). When woman lead, change happens. Retrieved from http://www.unaids.org/sites/default/files/media_asset/when-women-lead-change-happens_en.pdf

UNAIDS (2). (2018). Knowledge is Power. Retrieved from http://www.unaids.org/sites/default/files/media_asset/jc2940_knowledge-is-power-report_en.pdf

UNAIDS. (2017). Start free stay free AIDS free: 2017 progress report. Retrieved from http://www.unaids.org/sites/default/files/media_asset/JC2923_SFSFA_2017progressreport_en.pdf

UNAIDS (3). (2018). UNAIDS DATA 2018. Retrieved 15 March 2019. Retrieved from http://www.unaids.org/sites/default/files/media_asset/unaids-data-2018_en.pdf

UNAIDS. (2015). 2015 Progress Report on the Global Plan Towards the Elimination of New HIV Infections Among Children by 2015 and Keeping their Mothers Alive. Retrieved From www.unaids.org/sites/default/files/media_asset/JC2774_2015ProgressReport_GlobalPlan_en.pdf

UNAIDS. (2018). Miles to go: closing gaps, breaking barriers, rightening injustice. Retrieved from http://www.unaids.org/sites/default/files/media_asset/miles-to-go_en.pdf

UNFPA. (2016). Universal Access to Reproductive Health: Progress and Challenges. Retrieved 15 March 2019, from UNFPA (2016). Universal Access to Reproductive Healthcare: Progress and Challenges. Retrieved from https://www.unfpa.org/sites/default/files/pub-pdf/UNFPA_Reproductive_Paper_20160120_online.pdf

YOUR KNOWLEDGE HAS VALUE

- We will publish your bachelor's and master's thesis, essays and papers

- Your own eBook and book - sold worldwide in all relevant shops

- Earn money with each sale

Upload your text at www.GRIN.com
and publish for free